AGAINST ALL ODDS

AGAINST ALL ODDS

From the Jail Cell to Leather Chairs, My Story God's Glory

MYOSHI THOMAS

Printed in the United States of America

Published by AmplifyHer

Unless otherwise indicated, Scriptures are taken from the New King James Version of the Bible.

ISBN: 978-0-359-07462-4

First Edition

Dedication

This book is dedicated to my mom Helen Robinson-Rimmer. Thank You for loving me, being an awesome mother and for teaching me to never give up on my dreams. You taught me that when life throws you lemons to make lemonade.

To my wonderful and loving children Erin Robinson, Lamonica Robinson Quarshea Robinson and Shekithqua Jenkins. Thank you for helping to mold me into the woman that I am today.

Thank You for always understanding even when I didn't. Thank you for believing in me.

To my Mister Melvin Keith Thomas We did it Baby!!! Thank you for all the late nights and early mornings. Thank You for covering me and putting up with me during the birth of this book. I love you!!

CONTENTS

THE POWER OF PRAYER IS REAL

Chapter one

THE POWER OF PRAYER IS REAL

I remember going to prison like it was yesterday.

"You are now here by sentenced to 12 years hard labor. This is to be served at the Louisiana Correctional Facility for women."

Those words packed more power than I could have ever imagined.

I was numb...

I was hurt...

In that moment I refused to cry. I refused to breakdown in that courtroom.

I felt like I was standing alone. No one there.

Here I stand alone with no one there. I kept thinking to myself "How did I get here?"

All I could think about was my children. They were my world. My children were all that I had at this moment.

Let me tell you where it all began. I had my first daughter at a young age. At that time, I made a vow that I would do whatever it took to make sure that she was okay.

I had my mom, but she made it very clear that my daughter was my responsibility. I started hustling at a young age to provide for my daughter. While hustling and trying to make ends meet for my daughter I ended up having another baby. It was at that time that I made the choice to drop out of school in the tenth grade to take care of my children.

I was always attracted to older men because I felt like they were just more mature. My oldest children's father was older than me and I thought that he would be the answer to my dreams. Like most young girls I imagined having the white picket fence and a happy home.

Boy was I wrong. I learned early that I would have to do whatever it took to make sure that my children were okay because my dream was just that, a fantasy but not my reality.

I used to hear some females say that they were "KEPT women" and I used to wonder what they meant by that. I had always been drawn to the dope boys. Back where I grew up they were the ones who had it going on. I didn't realize that being a kept woman came with a price.

You had to deal with other women, jackers and the police. While I was being a kept woman in my relationships I started learning the tricks of the trade. I would watch the men whom I had relationships with, I watched how they ran their business.

I learned very early on that I had the mentality of a hustler. I made up in my mind that I could take care of me and my kids without having the added stress that my relationships were bringing. I have always been hard headed and for me to have to deal with outside foolishness wasn't for me.

I started out stealing but I quickly realized that it wasn't for me. I soon started writing checks and this became a habit for me. I opened banks accounts everywhere and it was on from there. It was like a job for me.

I get up like it was normal. Get dressed and go to the store to write checks. Never thinking it would catch up with me and take me away from my children. I was placed on probation for issuing worthless checks. It didn't stop me, I continued to go out and write bad checks. By the time I was on probation I had started writing them in other states. I was warned many times, but I think it was the rush or maybe the thrill of writing them. I learned that if you dress the part you can write a check and they wouldn't think twice.

I had furnished my entire house with fraudulent checks. I was purchasing the best of the best things for my children.

When it all falls down…

I soon found out that just when you think no one is watching, when you think you have it all together… You will be ambushed. ***I got pulled over on the way to work for a traffic stop and didn't see my children for seven years.***

Their fathers weren't in their lives on a regular basis. I was all that my children knew.

A routine day.

A routine traffic stop.

The road I had driven so many times.

That day changed my life forever.

I am forever grateful that my family stepped in to take care of my children during this time. I was so caught up in the street life. I wasn't trying to hear or listen to God.

My mom has always instilled God in us even though she raised us all by herself, she never allowed us to forget about God. I can honestly say it's because of my Mother's prayer that I am here today.

I was living the good life or so I thought. The life that I once knew was turned upside down and my kid's world destroyed because of my actions.

The ride to Louisiana Correctional for Women felt like the longest I had ever taken. I was riding up to a facility that would be where I would spend the next seven years of my life.

Here I would be for the next seven years of someone telling me what to do and how to do it.

Working for 4 cents a day in a hot or cold yard depending on the season. Having my family visit me in a crowded and loud gym. Not knowing if they would make it or even have minutes on the phone for me to call. Not knowing how this would affect my children in many ways even their adult life.

The holidays were the worst and the longest. During the holidays is when it seemed like the mail stopped.

There were many nights I laid in that ceil and cried because I knew the choices that I had weren't right. I knew I had to make them in order for my children to have a life.

I had never been away from my kids. Being surrounded by murderers and so far from what I knew as my life, it was in that jail cell that my life took a turn. In that jail cell is where God dealt with me and all my mess. It is there that God showed me Myoshi .

It wasn't a pretty sight either!

In that cell is where God broke me and started rebuilding me to who I am today.

I had to trust and believe that God would get me through the 7 years.

Prison, my wilderness...

Prison is not a nice place. You must sleep with one eye open for real. Here you encounter people from all walks of life. I now understand why I had to go through this but back then I had no clue. This is where my encounter with God took place.

Alone in a cell in my wilderness.

I must keep it real, I did not always look at this experience this way. I was upset with God. But I soon had to learn that this was my journey and that this was part of who I am today. I had to go through this to start my walk towards my destiny and purpose.

Encounters with God are not always nice or pretty He gets deep down and dirty pulls out everything that you think you have hidden. It was in that cell that God began to show me that

> " ***if you just surrender and do my will I will give you the desires of your heart***. If you will just move out the way and allow me to be the head of your life you will not lack anything. Just trust me."

It was an ugly mess, but I made it. Because of this experience I am here to tell you that obedience is better than sacrifice.

It is was in that jail cell in St. Gabriel La that God took me from frustration to favor.

You might wonder what I mean by that. Well, I was really frustrated with my life, how I was living and how it was affecting my children. I knew something had to change in order for my life to get better.

I just didn't want to change because I was comfortable with it. This was something that I was familiar with and comfortable doing. However, when God turns up the heat IT IS HOT!

God made me very uncomfortable and it caused me to do something quickly.

My freedom was at stake and I wasn't willing to gamble it. Let me tell you, when the checks started to get rejected the police were at my door every other day with a warrant for my arrest.

It was the feeling you have if you are staying with someone and instead of them asking you to leave they just make you so uncomfortable that you make the decision to leave. God allowed me to fall ON PURPOSE to get to my purpose on purpose.

If you are at a place where you want to know what God wants you to do you can simply ask Him and He will gladly tell you.

> If any of you lacks wisdom, you should ask God, who gives generously to all without finding fault, and it will be given to you. James 1:5

TRUSTING GOD WHEN IT FEELS THERE IS NO WAY

Chapter two

TRUSTING GOD EVEN WHEN YOU FEEL THERE IS NO WAY

Coming home from prison was not easy. Even though I had an education no one wanted to hire me because I would forever be considered an ex-con to the world.

When bills were due, and I had no food I had to trust and rely on God to make it through. I had to remind not only God but myself at times of His unchanging word. Standing on the word can be hard when you are struggling and see no way out. It's tempting to go back to what's easy to do to get what you need.

Even as I write this book and God has taken me back through this emotional journey I remember so clearly everything that I went through. I know for certain that it was trusting in God that got me through. I had to trust God with my life.

There were times when I reached out to so called friends thinking that they would come ... nothing, no reply, no call back. They turned their backs and talked about me and whatever situation I was going through at the time.

There were times when we went without lights, gas, water and only God made a way. I went to bed hungry many nights, but God made sure those kids had a meal. I can remember times when I felt like that my kids were better off without me because we were going through this and they didn't deserve it.

To hear them say "It's okay mama we are okay" still touches me to this day.

There have been times when I just didn't know how things would work out and I wanted to end it all because I didn't see any other options.

What do you do when it all comes falling on you?

See when I finally got it together and storms came raging I called on the Name of Jesus and He was there with no questions but all answers.

Trusting God even when you can't trace Him is a fact but the key to that is your Faith level?

Do you really Trust God when you can't see beyond what you see?

This reminds me of the story in the bible about the dry bones. You know when the spirit put you in a dry place. This is how I felt dead --no life. What is to come out of this? Prison is a very dark and dreary place many has lose hope and given up on life itself.

Standing on God's Word

Being obedient to His Word was most important. As I told you, obedience is better than sacrifice. When He told me to go a certain way I had to follow. I kept being on the Potter's wheel until I learned my lessons.

Until I was able to pass whatever test it was I couldn't move forward nor, would God allow me to prosper in any area. It was vital for me to pass the tests that I was put through.

There are times when you will be tried and tested to see if you are true. When I decided to just give it all to God it did not just stop there. I decided that I was not writing any more checks, I am not dealing with nothing that will take me back.

I was tested-- I remember it like it was yesterday. I now have three of my grandkids and Christmas was coming up and I didn't have anything. I was like ok I can go write a few checks and get the things they wanted (this was this flesh talking). You know when that devil wants you to do something he stays on you to do it. I had to stand on God's Promises and remind Him I have been Faithful and unmovable.
I am standing on your words. I am like the woman at the well if I can just touch the hem I will be healed. I had to have a made up and willing mind. I prayed, cried and fasted and God answered.

They had a Christmas! That situation reminded me that I knew the God I served. I got in the word and dedicated myself to understanding it. When I surrendered that's when I really started living life.

Falling in Love with Jesus was the best decision of my life. Having a servant's heart and being able to be led has helped me in so many ways. I was humbled when I went to prison.

People will never let you live certain things down. They will hold it over your head. I learned so much from not being able to rely on people. I had to change either what I was doing or how I was doing it and, in some cases, just let it go. There goes that word again ***Change***. Before I could trust, have faith or do anything with God I had to surrender to His will. I had to totally give myself away so that God could use me.

This is where I had to speak to the dry bones. The bible says Can these bones live? Ezekiel was told by God to Prophesy upon the bones. I had to take the grave clothes off. This is where I learned about living in the overflow.

Keep Moving...

I remember one time after getting out of prison when my boys and I attended an event out of town in Houston. As we were leaving the weather was getting bad and I don't like driving in the rain on the highway. As we headed out, I noticed a sign that said 70 miles. When we started out there was a light rain but as we continued it got heavier.

It was to the point that you couldn't see anything, and the windshield wipers combined with the air vent were still not helping much. I was about to call Mister (my husband) and tell him that we are going to wait it out and I heard God loud and clear say:

> **NO PUT ON THE HAZARD LIGHTS AND KEEP MOVING.** This is what is wrong with some people in the world today. When the storms of life come down heavy they want to stop or pull over until it stops or slows down.
>
> You have to keep moving you may be at a slower pace but you are still moving."

I was terrified while driving in the rain! I couldn't see anything, and the cars were flying past us. I wanted so badly to pull over but I put on my hazard lights and kept moving.

Despite wanting to just pull over and wait for the rain to pass, I kept pushing until I went beyond the storm. Once we hit the 70 mile mark right at the 71 mile mark there was the sunshine. 7 + 1 = 8 .

The meaning of 8 is new beginnings--when the storms of life come you want to pull over but you need to be ready to keep moving there is something greater when you withstand what was meant to take you out.

YOU PAST SHOULD NOT DICTATE YOUR FUTURE

Chapter three

YOU PAST SHOULD NOT DICTATE YOUR FUTURE

Throughout my journey I have learned that you cannot allow your past to stop you from achieving your dreams

This requires pushing past your fears and taking the leap. Leap into your dreams regardless what it looks like. It took me quite a bit of time to truly grasp this concept.

I had to start by breaking down what fear is to me. What am I afraid of?

What is this fear costing me?

My fear was about my past of being in prison. I was so worried about what people would think about me and say about me. Fear took my focus off what God had already spoken and shown me.

I had to push fear to the side because it made me stop looking at my situation with my spiritual eyes
I accepted my truth. Yes, I am a girl from the hood with big dreams. I am the same girl from that hood that went to prison. I am that same girl from the hood that came from the bottom to the top because of God's Mercy and Grace.

My past is just that, my Past. My being in prison is just part of my story this book is not done yet. Being in prison was painful for me but it was during this pain that my purpose was birthed. It was this experience that gave me the determination and motivation to push forward. This has helped me to keep moving even at times when I don't or didn't want to move.

This experience has been the fuel to my fire to let others know that it is ok to fall. To let others, know that sometimes your past is really directing you to your future.

I once heard a woman of God preach a message about the donkeys who will try to distract your assignment. She reminded me at that time of what I would like to remind you of. Those "donkeys" are simply directing you into your Purpose. If I would have never gone to prison I would have never gotten into position for my purpose.

I thank God for those donkeys and you should too! I never thought I would be telling my story to anyone. Now knowing that it would be able to give others hope or help them realize that there is life after prison. This journey has been incredible. I had to learn to take the steps to start working on my dreams. I have started setting goals both short and long term. My commitment has also been to be realistic about them.

You have so much power when you use your past as a guide and learning tool.
Don't get upset about your past...

Don't beat yourself up...

Your past should be a place to visit not a place to stay. Sometimes you must go there but you don't have to remain there. It is all part of the process. It is an examination and you know the teacher is always quiet during the test!

Even with everything stacked against you, you can make it.

Have you ever wondered what to do when your back is against the wall? For me my animal instinct kicks in like that of a lioness. I have learned to go into survival mode by any means necessary. Staying reminded that I can and will make it at all costs.

To get something, you never had you must go places that you have never been. For me it was in another place with God. That secret place with God where it was only us. That place where I wanted to be and just love on Him.

At one time the police were coming back to back with warrants for my arrest and I couldn't understand why. It was one day while sitting in the kitchen I heard God loud and clear say let me tell you why I allowed all that to happen.

> "It was necessary for your preparation. You had to be prepared for your assignments. I had to make sure you were equipped with the tools you needed to make the impact you are going to make.
>
> For you to speak on things I need you to go through them. You cannot speak on that which you haven't

been through and overcame. The things I have called you to do will come to pass. You had to be moved from the familiar to the unfamiliar. You had to be emptied so that I can use you. All old things needed to be done with.

These were old charges that were coming up and I was like when is it going to stop Lord. It was in these times that I wanted to just stop. I was discouraged, and it seemed like I was getting knocked down every time I tried to stand. While doing the right thing by God I felt it wasn't good enough. God spoke to me in that time that He needed me to have a clean slate and plate.

Against all odds God will get the Glory...

I was like the rose that grew from the concrete. I had to fight to blossom into this beautiful rose. I was tough trying to grow when all the conditions and the environment was seemingly coming against me.

Everyone was saying I wouldn't make it and that I would be back in prison. They kept telling me that if I did do something no one really support me. Yes, this discouraged me many times and in many ways but just like that rose I kept pushing because I knew there was better for me.

I felt like the Little Engine that could...I had to keep repeating, I think I can. The journey was sometimes ugly and dirty, but God cleaned me up and will clean you up. As you're getting cleaned up you will look and talk different.

My mindset had to change in order for me to see what God had for me. I had to be hungry for God and willing to do whatever it was that God needed from me whether I understood it or not.
So many people held the fact that I went to prison against me. I couldn't get a job because of my background but God said that if I will just Trust Him it would all work out!

I haven't worked a job for someone else since 2007. I trusted God and took a leap. All the Glory goes to God. Because of His mercy and grace, I made it on the other side. There were many times my back was against the wall and I was counted out, but Glory be to God He kept me in the race.

Even when I didn't care enough for myself or when I could not see the way. I was breaking through the concrete!

What man was saying was impossible God was showing that it was possible, if I would just give it to Him. All that I needed, and all that you need is a teaspoon of Faith, a tablespoon of willpower and a cup of courage.

You must make up your mind to start using the bricks that are thrown at you as stepping stones. The bricks that are thrown at you are meant to knock you out, but I caught them and created a pathway to my purpose and destiny. I had to learn that they were not meant for me to carry but to walk on. Now these bricks were heavy and many I couldn't carry because of the weight.

I had to push, pull and drag them. They were weighing me down and I could not understand why. I was mentally, emotionally and physically drained, but I kept pushing. My arms were heavy and full and instead of me just dropping them I continued to collect them as they were being thrown. Brick after brick...

"You will never be anything"

"You went to prison" ..." no one cares"

"You haven't changed"

"Who cares about your story?"

It was not until one day after church service I asked God How long will you allow me to suffer?

Let me tell you, the struggle was so real. I was barely making it and now on top of this my daughter is in the exact same place I was --Prison. I had to take on the responsibility of her children.

You see the pattern? Years ago, my mom had to do the same thing for me. I saw firsthand that generational curses are real. I had to break that curse for my grandkids and to save my children from going down that path of destruction.

This is where my mindset and thought process had to change. Being in prison taught me how to adapt to the environment. How to think outside of the jail cell and wall. The concrete wall.

I begin to place the bricks of shame, doubt, fear, guilt, and prison on the ground. I had to place them under my feet because carrying them was too much. I had to place them on the ground so that I could start this journey.

It started right there in that jail cell with the very first brick. Let it all go!!! This brick starts the first day of your new life. I had to use them to keep moving in spite of what it looked or felt like. These stepping stones I am using is to walk into my purpose and to help others know that it can be done. These bricks can be made into some very colorful and beautiful stepping stones in your garden of life. I learned that you can't heal what you cannot speak. The bricks can be turned into beautiful pieces of stones to build a lovely pathway. I had to change shoes because at first, I had to wear tennis shoes to run. Now I am stepping high in my heels on these bricks. No one can curse what His blood covers.

THE BEST REVENGE IS SUCCESS

Chapter four

THE BEST REVENGE IS SUCCESS

The Queen B said it best.

"Let your success announce you and make the noise." It is best to just show up and God will show out. Even writing this book was not in my plans but it was spoken over my life many times.

Fear was stopping me.

I know that my story will impact so many people, but I allowed fear of the unknown to stop me from doing what God had already told me to do. Even though I didn't take that jump God still pushed to move towards it.

Even when I didn't want to step out, I still felt the push. I had always felt comfortable working behind the scenes, but God wouldn't allow me to keep doing it. Eventually I started getting more and more invites for speaking engagements and to show up at women's conferences.

I would share encouraging social media posts and people started reaching out to me for words of encouragement or to just simply pray with and for them.

This was one of those moments when I realized that it was helping more than just me. I knew that I was determined and devoted to not give up. Especially when it felt that all odds were against me. I was the underdog, and many had counted me out but I kept standing on the fact that God counted me in.

I stopped allowing my focus to shift to my past. I had to keep my focus on what was in front of me and close the door on what was behind me.

I remember being in prison and there were so many fights.

When a fight would break out we had to get down and put our hands behind our heads until they got the situation under control. I learned something even reflecting on that.

It was the perfect snapshot of what this journey had become for me. When I felt like life was giving me the biggest fights, I had to get on my knees and stay there until God said it was clear to get up!

Many people said that I wouldn't and couldn't make it. They said that I would forever be an ex-con but I put my shades on and faced every struggle, setback disappointment, let down regret and heartache face on.

Now I let my education, knowledge and wisdom do the talking. I allow the God in me to introduce me!

I shifted into letting my success become the revenge not me. It is never okay to allow anyone to take you back to a level you already graduated from.
I had to start reminding myself and I am reminding you to depend on the Lord in whatever you do, and your plans will succeed Proverbs 16:3

STOP BEATING YOURSELF UP ABOUT YOUR PAST

Chapter five

STOP BEATING YOURSELF UP ABOUT YOUR PAST

One of the best changes in my mindset took place when I realize that there is a lesson in your struggle.
I have learned so many lessons from my struggles.

They have taken me to some dark place and dark times in my life. However, the sun did shine again after I mastered and truly learned the lessons. Some tests and storms have made me strong and wise. It was during these times that I had to be taught by the master (God).

This is where I learned that I was teachable and the fundamentals of being teachable. Even though I was battered I wasn't shattered and could still be used. God knew I was useable, but I had to let God know I was available.

You are still useable but until You say Father here I am to worship you and I am available, God will not move.
He will wait on you!
When you think that you are waiting on God, you must realize that there are times when God is waiting on you to become obedient and available.

I can say this because I know for certain if it had not been for God I would have lost my mind in prison or spent my life in prison. My relationship with God has continued to go to another level.

I had to endure a season of transition and change. It felt like everything around me was going crazy, my children, husband, family. It was during this season that I had to just surrender and give it all to God.

It was during this time that my whole life changed. I learned that a change is not a change until you and I change.

My mess was so ugly and stinky but God said “I allowed it” . He did this so that He could get the Glory.

Understanding this made the tough moments and seasons times that I exchanged my will to embrace His will. My life hasn’t been the same!

Again, it is not easy and many times I feel alone because many don’t understand me at times, but it is okay because I know that it is all working together for the good. It is not always for others to understand me but to see the God in me. It is for me to stay the course and run the race that God has before me.

It is for me to show others what’s to come when your past pushes you into your future. It is for me to be a walking billboard for Christ. The struggles have taught me some very valuable lessons. They have taught me how to deal with things from different views. They have taught me that things don’t always look like they seem. The struggles of life will teach you some very valuable lessons. If you open your mind and heart, God will do just what He said He would. I am living off of the Promises of God.

Let the struggles teach you your next lesson. Your destiny is not a matter of chance but a matter of choice

Let the luggage go…

The luggage of the past will keep you in the past if you allow it to. I love the song Bag Lady:

> "Bag lady you gone hurt your back
> Dragging all them bags like that"

I was dragging my bags because that is how much I had. I mean I did not even know the weight of the stuff until I started unpacking it. I didn't realize how much damage baggage could cause. Carrying all of my baggage made me physically sick and it was draining me.

Not only did I have my baggage but other people's baggage as well. I had backpacks, duffle bags and carry on suitcases. It was like I was at the airport holding the line up because it all had to be checked.
Imagine that.

I had to stop and take inventory of my baggage before reclaiming my bags. Imagine the time that it took to dump all those bags and begin the process of seeing what I needed to pack.

I had to remove, throw away and repack my baggage. I had to question myself during this process.

Did this baggage even serve a purpose for me?

Is this baggage worth paying a fee for?

What is the weight of this baggage?

Forgiving was a big thing for me and it was the heaviest of my baggage. It was during this time that I learned that two of my biggest bags were forgiving and holding on to my past. I was labeled as damaged goods. I had to look through all of this damage and determine what was worth saving.

I should have taken the time out to deal with the baggage. Unfortunately, I didn't. I kept moving like things were alright and kept adding to it.

Before I could continue this journey, I had to go through the damaged baggage and give what could be fixed to God.

Forgiving others for what they had done and most of all forgiving myself for making the mistakes that I made. I had to learn to give my baggage to God to carry. God says cast all your cares upon Him. He is our burden carrier. I had to learn that God is our first defense against baggage.

I didn't turn to God because I felt like my sins made me unworthy. I felt like I didn't deserve another chance because of all the other chances He had given me time after time.

My sins kept me from the source of help that could truly lighten my load. I had to shift my mindset and make God my number one baggage carrier.

The tongue in your shoe should be bigger than the tongue in your mouth

.These words were spoken at an event that I attended. I have always been told that you get back what you put in so I am constantly attending events and opportunities that will help me grow.

I am always willing to learn something. I went to an event for one of my businesses and it was simply amazing. Being in the room with women who were successful and didn't mind helping you get the tools you needed to get to where you were going in this business felt incredible.

Let me be transparent for a moment. It was truly a culture shock to me because I was unfamiliar with this type of environment. I knew that God had been preparing me for something, but I didn't realize that this was it. Not until I was back in my room in the bathroom crying my eyes out because I was so Grateful and Thankful for this chance!

Meaning my circle was changing and God was showing me what success really looked like. There was 600 women at this event and they were movers and shakers in this business.

One of the speakers was a fireball and on point with her message. Mrs. JP spoke these profound words that stuck with me and I didn't realize how they would impact me until we started brainstorming for this book.

"Your shoe tongue size should be bigger than the tongue in your mouth."

This just kept ringing in my head and I was like ok God what are You telling me?

What is it that you want me to take from these words?

God has a peculiar way of talking to me.

The mouth is a dangerous thing and can be detrimental. The power of life and death lies within the tongue. When you speak something, you must be careful because it will go forth.

The tongue in your shoes holds the shoe together and it enables the shoes to be tied and worn comfortably. The tongue in your mouth controls or allows words to be spoken. Now the tongue in your shoes should be bigger than the tongue in your mouth. To me this means that you must be mindful of the what you say from your mouth.

Words can be damaging and very destructive.

The tongue in your mouth is the root of your mouth.

Just like the tongue in the shoes holds the shoe together. The tongue in your mouth holds your mouth. Proverbs 18:7 KJV reminds us that “a fool’s mouth is his destruction and his lips are the share of his soul”

Learn to block out the negative of words spoken from your past

Sometimes it is hard to move past the negative things that people say about you and in most cases to you. For me it kept me in a place of darkness until I learned how to run to my

secret place. It kept me unable to move forward and to see myself the way that God saw me.
It used to truly hurt the more that people tried to down talk me and remind me of what they thought I would never be capable of doing.
From the time I set foot on free ground I worked so hard to prove myself. It felt like I had a target on my back because I went to prison. What I found to be empowering was that while society would try to call me an Ex-con, God saw something different.

The very experience that seemed like it would tear me down, God used that very thing to raise me up. I believe the same is true for you. The labels that you thought could be used to disqualify you will be the very label that God can use to qualify you.

I had to get it in my soul that I am who God says I am. A reminder of this for me is Proverbs 18:21 death and life are in the power of the tongue; and they that love it shall eat the fruit thereof.
You will eat what you speak...

My mindset shifted when I shifted. There is no way you will stay or think the same when God moves you.

Moving meant getting around positive-minded people who are not only going in the direction that I desire to go, but those that are already where I desire to be. As the saying goes, if you want to be a Millionaire get around millionaires.

Therefore, I had to be around business owners, stock brokers, bankers, real estate agents for this to become my own normal. The results of your future are a product of what you speak or hear whether good or bad today.

God will use the very thing that others thought would break you to build you up and bless you. Make the decision to guard what you listen to, stay away from the negative talk, and make efforts to speak blessings over yourself. Yes, there were many days when I had to encourage myself on this journey. The I AM works for me and I speak them daily
... I AM a Queen
... I AM beautiful

Speak the word of God over your life!

REAL SISTERHOOD

Chapter six

REAL SISTERHOOD

I just shared with you how important it was for me to start moving forward in my life. When you are moving in life there is no doubt that your circle will surely change.

Your outlook on things will be much clearer and what worked in the past will not work as you progress towards your more amazing future. You will be more focus driven and your passion will blossom.

You will find that you will start being around those who truly have your best interest at heart.
Before I started this journey, I thought that I had a solid team. That was until God started blessing and elevating me. At that time many were exposed and removed.

I learned that on the way up requires cuts. It hurt but some are not meant to move with you as you elevate to the next season or level. I learned that holding onto things that were no longer necessary caused me more harm than good. Holding on was the very thing that prevented me from moving.

Everyone is not meant to go to the next level with you when God is elevating you. A powerful speaker Tony Gaskins said it best, separation before elevation is a must. You must be around people who are positive and will push you to the next level. Get around those who will tell you the truth not just what you want to hear. Like-minded people who share life time goals with each other are the types of circles that you want to be in.

Having someone there to catch you when you fall. Being in a place of peace is so amazing but having those around you who are willing to help you get to where you are trying to go is everything!

Real Sisterhood is being your sister's keeper.

Feel what she feels..

Going through with your sister with no regrets or ulterior motives.

I can say that those that have been on this ride me with me have been in the mud with me. The good, bad and the ugly. They have fed me, clothed me, prayed for me when I couldn't for myself.

I have never heard anger around not one of the things that they have done.

Everyone does not deserve access to your destiny. People only throw shade because you are shining bright, this means get around people who will cause you to keep shining!
You cannot share your million-dollar dream with ten cent minded people. People will never understand your vision because it wasn't given to them so therefore they will not see it and will laugh at you until it because a reality and then if they're not meant to be in your circle, the hating will begin.

If you desire to see your circle change, it's important that you become the type of person that you want to be around.

Someone who is willing to celebrate the success of others. This is a must.

Having a sister circle is a wonderful thing. The event that I attended with the 600 women was everything in every essence. It was in this moment that I knew I made the right choice and that they are truly their Sister's Keeper. That this sister circle is unbreakable and unshakeable.

I have learned that you have to be careful and watchful because all smiles are not smiles but upside down frowns. Those that say they celebrate you are not always being honest. I finally understand what my
mom meant when she instilled this in us. I learned that when you celebrate someone else God will move for you.
I remember a time when it seemed that everyone around me was being blessed. I was genuinely happy for them. They cried, and I cried! They were excited, and I was excited.

Before I knew it, God had Blessed me. This is all about being real and having that agape love for your sister. In my circle if one wins we all win. We all are going to eat and be happy and I mean we really celebrate each other.

I try to do something monthly to celebrate and let my sisters know that I love them, and I want to give them their roses while they are living. With celebrating each other comes empowerment and encouragement to help each other to evolve.

In a real sisterhood your goal is to help each sister to take that jump or step because many are not ready to jump. Many of us need encouragement to move past whatever holds us back. My friend/mentor is the one that took that step to push me to evolve into who I am today. She involved me in every event she had and made sure I spoke at each one. This opened many doors for me to share my story.

I had to learn that when so called sisters couldn't celebrate me publicly, it was because they were tearing me down privately. They had to whisper my celebration because it wasn't real. At this event with all these black successful ladies the love was real and felt. Sister in success, I am my sister's keeper!

BOSS…—Building Other Sister's Steps—

Most people use the word Boss to mean that they have it going on or they are the Boss. There are a lot of meanings for the word boss—

> a person in charge of a worker or organization, giving someone orders in a domineering manner and excellent;

outstanding is the definition the dictionary gives.

I wanted to know what God's meaning of Boss was. He took me to: Thessalonians 5:11 Therefore encourage one another and Build each Other up.

This was powerful because it showed me that being a Boss is more than just being over something. It's about being here to uplift, encourage and to motivate each sister to become positive, productive and to walk in their purpose.

I want my sisters to know their own truth and their whys of life. At the sisterhood event that I attended I remember hearing the statement "Your Whys should make you cry. "

There are steps to get to where God is taking us so therefore we must be a bridge for the next sister to cross over into her land of honey. We must be willing to stand in the gap for and with our sisters. We must help each other get prepared for what is to come.

It is time for us to come together and stop tearing each other down. Being a boss means to start lifting up and truly celebrating our sisters. Sisterhood is a wonderful thing when it is true. I am surrounded by some very powerful women and I Thank God for them. Each one of them have helped to serve as my stepping stones.

What you overcame just might be the stepping stone that your sister needs to complete, add or even start her pathway. Make the decision to be a BOSS: Build Other Sister's Steps

Caked Up ...

Most people think about material things or money when you say caked up. I heard a Man of God once say "God will lock you up sometimes in order to set you free "

Another lesson that I learned in while being in my own sister circle was about being successful in the business industry. A speaker shared the principle of baking a cake.

Even though these were the keys for success in business they are can be applied or used to be successful in life.

Eggs: a strong why- why are you where you are in life? Why aren't you moving? What is your why?

Flour: hunger- Are you hungry enough to follow your dreams? What is your hunger level? What are you willing to do to eat?

Milk: ambition and passion- how driven are you? What risk are you willing to take to achieve your goals and dreams? What are you passionate about doing?

Butter: Coachability and humility- are you willing and able to be trained? Are you able to listen with an open mind and not be combative? Can you take constructive criticism?

Sugar: morals values and ethics - in life these three little things carry major weight. In order to be successful in anything you do you must have these. If you don't stand for something you will fall for anything.

Baking soda- the ability to manage your emotions. Understand that every action does not require a reaction. Pick your battles wisely because in most cases all you need to do is stand. God is or has already fought it and won.

Service: stay in your own lane. Serve with a good heart and watch God move. I have a heart to serve and give and sometimes I get hurt but I have learned to keep moving. Most of all I Trust God,
I know that life can be a process just like baking a cake! You put all the things in a bowl, mix it and pour it in a pan and let it bake...

I remember my granny always saying sit down somewhere before you make my cake fall. After you have put all together never be afraid to let go and let God bring it all together.

You are now caked up! You just made this cake from scratch. This is not a box cake. A box cake only allows you to add a few things but that homemade cake requires you to use everything you have, to make it.

You leave one thing out and it is ruined. This is how it is when you are serving God there is no half baking. You cannot keep open and closing the oven door.

These are lessons that I've learned in my sister circle and being surrounded by those who will push you higher will bring more life lessons your way as well.

FINDING TRUE LOVE

Chapter seven

FINDING TRUE LOVE

Loving yourself and knowing your self-worth is a journey. It was an emotional rollercoaster for me. I had to spend some time alone with myself to find out who Myoshi really was.

What did love really mean to me?
Was I even worthy or capable of being love?
What did true love look like?

I had to learn what I was looking for in life. Most importantly I had to learn my worth. It took me down a very dark path.

It was during these times that I learned to love the skin that I am in and I didn't have to use my body to get what I wanted.

I knew I always wanted to be married and have a family but before I could get there I had to be prepared. I had to ask myself questions that required me to dig deep inside to draw out the real me. Let me tell you, it was ugly.

When dealing with your true self you will have to deal with all the roads including the detours and curves up ahead. One of my detours seemed to be relationships.
The guys that I dated and had long term relationships with always seemed to be blocked from marriage.
There was always something standing there in the way.

The detour began in my mind thinking that it wasn't meant for me to be married. I took notice that I got to a point where I was not willing to treat or give a boyfriend a husband title. The more I began to love myself the more I recognized that I wasn't a doormat and wasn't going to be treated like one.
I am now so thankful to God for not answering some of those relationship prayers. I learned that some relationships are there to simply teach a lesson. They are just like the seasons, only for a moment.

It was very important for me to know who I was in order to know what I needed or wanted out of someone else. I learned that if you don't know who you are people will push their self on you. If you have no idea of who you are you will just follow and have no voice which can lead to a life you hate.

I needed a plan of action. Being in prison taught me how to stand up for myself and never settle for less. First, I had to stop letting what others thought of me or said about me have an effect. I had to look myself in the mirror and go back to those I AM daily affirmations. I started seeing myself how God sees me.

True love is when you can love yourself flaws and all. Imperfection is what makes us perfect within ourselves. Looking in that mirror on a consistent basis allowed me to begin to embrace my whole self.

Learning how to be loved...

Love is an action word and sadly sometimes it is rarely shown. I must admit that I am a hopeless romantic.
I like flowers, long walks in the park and sitting by the water.

It's the small things that matter for me. My relationship experience when dealing with someone from the streets was that they showed love totally different.

Although I had this vision in my head it didn't became a reality until I ran into Mister, my now husband. It taught me that you must be prepared and able to accept love.

There is so much more to the word love. You must love with no restrictions. Love beyond the hurt, unworthiness, self-doubt, the past. There were some things that I had to do for myself to know how to be loved. I learned a lot from my Ex's that I applied to my life when it came to my dating life.

These lessons became my blueprint to follow. I like to call them the five BE's to my life.
#1 Be Authentic
#2 Be My Best Self
#3 Be Confident
#4 Be Open
#5 Be Happy

This was my blueprint to learning how to be loved.

Mr. Right—"Hey Mr. what your name is!!!"

Growing up most of us dream and basically build our Mr. Right. He is the perfect man in your head. However, in reality it took me a few relationships and heartaches to get to him.

To be transparent for a moment, my Mr. Right was there all along, but I overlooked him because I had the man that I wanted in my head. A man in a uniform with an education and good credit. Now there were a few that I thought were Mr. Right but God always exposed them. Before I knew that I carried a mantle God protected and kept His hand on me. What could have felt like rejection was truly God's protection.

Now the relationships that I had helped me in various ways that I didn't know until God allowed me to see it all unfold. Each one played an important role when it came to preparing me for Mr. Right.
Things like cooking, cleaning, balancing a checkbook, and many do's and don'ts of relationship.
This was all preparing me for marriage.

My Mr. Right is from the streets but has swag. He was my middle school sweetheart. While we were growing up, when I couldn't get off the porch he used to bring me candy. I remember those moments, so when we reconnected and exchanged numbers, the rest was history.

God has a way of putting the pieces together. I say that because we both were broken when we reconnected. My Mr. Right is everything that I prayed for in a husband. Let me keep it real thought, it took much prayer and fasting to get us here to where we are today. Forgiving played a major role in us moving forward and keeping God first.

Mr. Right accepts my flaws and all but most of all he completes me. I never had anyone to not only pray with me but for me. He stands when I can't or don't have my strength. He is my covering, confidant and comfort. No matter how far-fetched my ideas may seem, he is right there to catch me if I fall, celebrate me when I step out and together we are making memories.

God made no mistakes with this one. He keeps me in tune and in check when it comes to the matter of the heart.

I love my husband and when we first started dated I always played the song Dreaming because it fits us so perfectly. We have been through a lot together, taken some losses together and we still remain together. I am his rib and it fits perfectly. We are not perfect, but we are perfect for each other. The more that I accepted and celebrated my own imperfections the more that I was able to open up to someone else.

Even through the hard times we push and keep the Faith. Keeping God first has been the glue for our marriage and the foundation for finding true self love and love in general for me.

Praying in preparation…

I have always had a prayer life even when I was doing wrong. During my sins I knew God had His hands on me and it was something that He wanted me to do. It wasn't until I surrendered to God and allowed Him to have His way that I started to see the vision.

I used to call them dreams until my Apostle told me that they were visions and God will be using me. Now like most people it went in one ear and out the other, until He started waking me up in the midnight hours to write things down.

I have always had a servant's heart and a giving spirit. I will give my last, but I had to learn that it is okay to say no because you can't sow into unfruitful grounds.

This is when and where I learned about the discernment spirit that I carry. I see and hear things and for quite some time I wasn't obedient to God when I was told to release things to people. I was like God these people are going to think I am crazy and question who I am.

It was at a women's conference at church that a woman spoke these words to me

> "you have not been obeying God, when God tells you to speak you do it.. I see you in a field of blooming flowers which represent your passion for helping young girls. I see you on a platform sharing your story. "

As she was saying this I knew that it was not a coincidence. I had just had the vision about me being on stage but not fully understanding it until now—years later.

I had been praying all this time before even knowing the vision or the impact and the effect my story would have on others. Not knowing the doors that would be opened to even allow me to stand on my story and boldly share it without being ashamed or guilty.

I have so many journals that I have kept over the years with things that God had me to write. The ones that touch me the most are my prayer requests for the new year. As I sit here typing the tears are literally rolling down my face because God is Faithful and will do just what He says He will do.

As I checked things off that have come to pass it is amazing. Another thing I do is when a prophet speaks something into my life I write it down and date it because when they are in the spiritual realm they don't remember what they tell you.

Even now when God allows or tells me to release something to someone and it comes to pass, and they call to give me a praise report I don't remember what I said to them.

Make the vision plain. I don't care how crazy it seems write it down and prepare, and watch God bring it to fruition.

BEING BOLD

Chapter eight

BEING BOLD

I have always liked being in the background. Working behind the scenes. Titles or having to have recognition is not important to me especially while doing God's business. I have been blessed to be surrounded by some very powerful women that are on the battlefield for the Lord.

These women are my covering and they speak things daily into my life. One of them spoke something to me about a year ago and it literally changed my world. She told me it's time for you to come from behind the scenes. It's time for you to be introduced to the world. You cannot stay in the background when God is pushing you to the front. God is about to make you known for your work. You are going to run things.

I was in awe because I was in the process of doing some things differently. I don't like attention, so I don't put myself in situations that will bring attention. I just wanted to do what God told me to do.

Boldly, standing in my now ...

I have been around those who no push me to be bold and stand in my now. I am learning how to use my past to inspire others who don't think they can live past their past.

It took me a minute to get to this place in my life because I was always worried about what others thought or said about me. Especially when it came to my past. Others have used my past to hurt or slander my name.
What others thought was for the bad, God has turned it around for my good and made it my platform. It became my stage and voice to show others that a past is simply that the past.

To show others that if God can do it for me surely, He will do it for them is so rewarding. That is when the breakthrough comes.

This can't happen until you are be bold enough to say That I am who God says I Am. I learned to embrace my individuality and uniqueness.

I now stick to my 3 C's of boldness. Confidence, Composure and Commitment.

Step out of your comfort zone…

I had to get uncomfortable to progress to the next level. I had to step outside the box and do things that I normally wouldn't do or even think of doing. This is where I learned about taking chances and risks.

This is where I gave God my all and used everything in me to worship and praise Him. I became a radical for God. God made me so uncomfortable with things that I had to start to do things differently. My mindset had to change for me to see the things that I was believing God for.

My mindset had to match my Faith. My Faith had to match my Trust in God. My Trust in God had to match my Belief in God. My Belief in God had to line up with the Word of God. I had to get a tune up to make sure my alignment was in line with God.

The things that I once felt were of importance no longer matter to me. This is where the shift came.
With shifting comes changes and with changes comes differences. Outlooks and outcomes become bold and wiser. I stepped out my comfort zones many times and the rewards were mind blowing. Stepping out my comfort zones helped me birth this book. It has been there, but I was afraid of failure or no support but was I ever wrong.

Follow your dreams…

Dream follower that is me. I have always dreamed big and had a big wild heart. While dreaming big I have learned that you cannot allow others to determine your dream.
I allowed fear to keep me from following my dreams and doing what God had already prepared for me. Fear of who would and wouldn't support me, fear of what they will say and most of all fear of failure.

It wasn't till I got in that place with God that nothing but pleasing Him mattered and fear no longer existed. I know longer worried about those things. I had to be prepared to take my rightful place on the Throne. I had to turn my dreams into goals and write them down. They had to be realistic and attainable.

Another shift happened when I learned about the power of vision boards. They are real, and they do work if you do the work. I do one every year and I am so amazed when I go back and see all the things that I can check off the board. With my goals I can implement my dreams and the vision board is to keep it in my eyesight to stay focused on it. When I found out who I was, accepted my dream, made goals, got the education and training to become successful I became Unstoppable and you can too!

GET INVOLVED

Chapter nine

GET INVOLVED

If you can't tell already it was a journey for me when it came to me sharing my story with other. We all know that people can be very judgmental. There are people who have the tendency to throw your past up in your face or will not let you to live beyond it.

I remember all the embarrassment that I carried with my past. It wasn't until someone who saw the greatness in me asked me to speak at an event she was having that my things started changing. I was taken aback and wondered "What am I going to say?" ... "Who is going to listen to me ?" and "How will my story help them?"

Little did I know that this was the first step to set me on this path. Little did I know that my story impacted the whole room. Little did I know it inspired people. That is when it hit me. You are an inspiration!

Inspiration is something that makes someone want to do something or that gives someone hope. This gave me the courage to create a force that would inspire someone else. Following the blueprint that God designed for me has opened many doors that I never dreamed or imagined would happen for me. The girl from the hood.

John-Quincy Adams stated: " If your actions inspire others to dream more, learn more, do more and become more you are a leader."

I share my store because I want people to know that it is real. If it inspires them to dream more and do more, with or without the title I know that it's worth it.

Yes, the struggles of life are real but my mission is to show that if you grab hold of God's right hand He will lead you. If you just allow God to order your steps you will not go wrong. Yes, you will be tested and tried but there is nothing too hard for God.

Your dream can become a reality...

If you dream it you can achieve it.

I remember growing up and seeing nice cars and houses. I would tell myself that I was going to have these things one day. Telling myself that I would own my own business when I grew up felt right. These are things that I spoke when I was young not knowing that I was speaking them over my life.

The power of the tongue! I knew I needed a plan. I think big so when I would speak big dreams to small minded people they would try to make me give up on my dreams. I call them dream killers.

They didn't have any dreams, so they tried to kill mines. This taught me to keep my mouth shut and let God speak for me. I don't allow myself to think small, everything must be grand. My mindset changed and so did my outlook on things. I started thinking one way and my lifestyle and living changed to that of my mindset. It was stated to me that you become that which you think you are. I had to readjust my mindset to align with God's plan. When you understand this you will start to see that your dreams can become your reality.

If you fall you can always get back up.

Failure was my biggest fear. The fear of not being good enough or not being what others thought was good enough, bothered me.

I realized however that failing is nothing to fear because you can always get back up after a fall. Most of time when you get back up you get up stronger and wiser. You get up having learned something from that fall.

God allows you to fall so that you can fall into that season or assignment that He needs us in. Meaning had I not gone to prison I wouldn't be able to tell my story of how I overcame when all the odds were against me.

I had to fall so that the fall could be effective. This is something to praise God for right here! It was necessary for God to get the Glory. It was needed for the preparation of what I am now birthing.

Share with those who are feeling hopeless

My prayer is that this book will help others with their journey and walking in their purpose. I once was hopeless, but I met someone who introduce me to Jesus and my life has never been the same.

Many people thought that I was crazy, or this was an act of some sort. My life took a whole 180-degree turn. There are many areas that I am not able to speak on because I didn't experience them. I am here to tell you boldly that I can speak to you about overcoming and moving forward against all odds.

I can tell you about putting your trust in God and Him working it out for your good. I can tell you about being in your wilderness and it is in that place where God will begin to use you if you are available. I can tell you that when you surrender and say yes to God you will be tested.

I can tell you that if you stay the course it is rewarding and worth it. There is hope in Jesus. I can tell you if your heart is pure, God will use you to reach other people and I can tell you that God choses you and He qualify the ones He calls. I can tell you that there is nothing too bad that God can't fix it and still use you. A broken crayon can still color!

"I have told you these things so that in Me you may have peace. In this world you will have trouble. But take heart! I have overcome the world." John 16.33

THE SOURCE

Chapter ten

THE SOURCE

If you have not gotten the full picture yet, I hope that you understand how your environment plays a role in moving forward against all odds. You have to stay connected to the SOURCE and people who will constantly point you back to God.

Staying plugged into the source was very important to me and my success. I had to surround myself with positive people and things.

You must surround yourself with people that will help you get to that next level. People who will motivate and encourage you to keep moving.

I remember meeting a family that loves God and trusted God no matter what came their way. I was so impressed by it and thought that I would like that type of relationship with God. So, I connected with them!

I have met some very powerful women and men of God. Some that have spoken many things in my life. They play very vital roles in my marriage and in how I handle things in our business. God was preparing me for the things to come in my life through this family. I watched, and they taught me so much and when I look back it was all necessary.

I have met two of the most amazing leaders through this family that I am forever grateful and thankful for. They have prayed me through many things. They hold me accountable for my actions. The best part is that they keep me plugged in to the source. My apostle, my teacher, my ear and shoulder to lean on is simply amazing and she loves God. She tells it like it is and if the Holy spirit didn't or don't speak it nor does she. I had to surround myself around God fearing people to understand and see the goodness of God.

I know some are wondering what does that mean? What it means is that I have always known about God but didn't always know God. I had to learn and know God for myself. My Apostle has taught to study to show thyself approved. It is so true! I had to have a relationship with God for myself. My church is my foundation and rock that has help me to develop in my walk with God. It is where I lay naked before God and my church family. This is where my burdens are laid. My church is my covering.

Fasting and worshipping will get you through so much! I will be the first to say and admit that it took me a minute when it came to fasting. My first time fasting almost took me out. I wasn't used to not eating and I couldn't figure out for the life of me what was the reason for this. It took God to gracefully break me in order to understand the concept of fasting and worshipping God.

It is important to study the word for yourself. This is not always easy. It is more than simply not eating or drinking. It is about your spiritual being and believe it or not it is about obedience.

Through fasting I learned discipline and self-control. This is where my dependence on God took place with each fast it got deeper. During my fast is when my transformation took place.

It is during my fast that what was in me started to come up and out.

Many ugly things were revealed and released during my times of fasting. I was so hungry for God that my mind would be so focused on Him that nothing else even mattered. I am a worshipper and will worship God all day long.

I came to know that when you worship God He will move and that sometimes your worship shifts things and situations. I know countless times when my back was against the wall, I would worship and fast and God would step right on in.

I know that when attacks, tests or setbacks come I must call on God. Many times, God has spoken to me so clearly. If you just worship Him that thing will be done. When I did what was asked of me God moved on my prayer request. It works if you truly depend and trust God. You must get out of your own way and let God have his way.

Your tithes and offering will open doors for breakthrough

I know that not a lot of people want to talk about this. I must be honest at one point I didn't either. I didn't want to give a single penny. I felt that it was my money and why should I take care of the preacher?

Oops did I just write that…

It is my truth. I thought that pastors are already living a good life so my money wouldn't make a difference.

My first mistake.

I soon started giving $5, $10 $15 and sometimes $20 depending on what I needed it for. I thought that this was enough until I attended an event that addressed this.

I heard a breakdown of what it means to bring the food to the storehouse and will a man rob God.

Second mistake.

I was convicted by this message. So, convicted that I asked God "Will a man rob God?". The answer forever changed me when it comes to tithes and offering. I heard Him loud and clear. YOU ARE.

I was floored. While I thought that I was paying my tithes, God had to show me that I was simply giving left overs. Now this had me feeling some type of way.

God spoke to me:

> "The first 10 percent, your first fruits. I don't give you half answered prayers, miracles signs or wonders. I give you my best and I want your best. You say you trust me but your actions says otherwise. I tell you to sow 100 you sow 10, you were disobedient."

This shook me because He was speaking so clearly. From that day I made a commitment to tithe off of everything that I get. I don't care if a bill is due I trust God enough to know that He keeps a ram in the bush. I can never repay God for all He has done for me, but I know my tithes and offering is a gift and God loves a cheerful giver. I know that sowing seeds on good soil will reap rewards.

Stand in the realm and place where God has you

The places where we are right now in life is where God wants us. This is the place where He is going to use us for His purpose. It is in this place that God starts revealing His plan.

You know God is truly amazing and when He starts showing you things you will be in awe of God.

Prayer changes things. I have always been the type of person where I needed to see things take place. I would say "God if this is of you or you talking to me show me." God began to show me. It was at the alter at church when I experienced the full effect of this.

In that special place with God at His feet. That secret place where you just allow God to use you. I know it is not easy, it is a battle daily. However, when you allow God to step in you can and will be able to stand.

A FAMILY THAT PRAYS

Chapter eleven

A FAMILY THAT PRAYS

When Family is Your Strength

I have no idea where I would be if it had not been for the bold prayers of my mother. Helen Robinson Rimmer, I could write a book just on how she has carried her children when we couldn't carry ourselves.

I watched my mom growing up denying herself to make sure that her children were taken care of. I watched my mom go to work rain, sleet, shine or snow.

We have our ups and down like any mother daughter relationship but her love for her children never changes. My mom made struggle look like it didn't exist. She raised us in a household by herself. She raised us with a strong and stern hand. She instilled moral values, ethic and character in each of her children.

She is a woman that loves God and I know that she is the apple of God's eye. She is a woman of courage and wisdom. I share this with you because my mother is the reason for the boldness that I have today. I am a firm believer that I am living off of many of my mom's prayer.

She stood in the gap for me when I didn't or couldn't stand for myself. She has wiped many tears from my eyes and cheered me on when I felt down.

The lessons that I have learned from my mother that I would pass on to you today will make a difference if you are serious about moving against all odds.

My mother taught me that when life gets you down you don't stay there, get yourself up and try again. She doesn't allow us to take anything for granted in life. Most importantly she often reminds me that life is short and it's vital to live it to its fullest.

The power of cover girls

My baby sister is a handful, but I couldn't imagine life without her. She has been an inspiration to me in so many ways. I love her for her drive and determination. She is the type of person that will strive for the best no matter how things look. I love her for her dedication.

Like many sisters we have our days and moments, but the love and loyalty has never been changed or been questioned. She has always been my cheerleader with whatever I have done in life. She has supported and encouraged me to move when I didn't have the strength and courage to do it myself. She is my cover girl.

The saying that it takes a village is so true. It has taken a village of Godly woman to keep me focused but most of all to embrace and help me evolve.

You may be familiar with the term Covergirl. These are the women who are typically rich with beauty. When I say this I'm not referring to riches and beauty. What I've learned in this journey is that I have needed cover girls who are willing to cover me! Who are willing to cover me in prayer, to cover me in encouragement.

My cover girls are like Jochebed who know that it takes a village to raise a child. These are truly my cover girls. I am talking about the definition of cover:

> to put something over, on top of, or in front of something else especially in order to protect, hide, or close it. : to be spread over or on top of (something).

I am talking about the type of women who are protectors over their homes, their families, their friends, and even their enemies. Cover girls don't mind helping others.

My cover girls are like Ruth dedicated, selfless, compassionate and generous. They are Kingdom Builders who will walk that walk. God knew that I needed them and still to this day because they are my check and balance system.

Let me tell you, I have a diverse group of sisters and I love them all. To be honest having sisters around you that believe in you is everything. If you have not found any yet, I encourage you to get around your cover girls!

How to face chastisement & sternness

This is dedicated to my brother whom I hold close to my heart. Really, he is my heartbeat. My mom's only son and I promise he thought that he was our daddy.

Let me tell you a little about my Smiley. I knew that he would be something great because at an early age he had hustle. He has always been business minded and knew how to save money. To know him you must first understand him. How he comes off can be perceived as being cocky, but it is really confidence and what he has been through to get to where he is now.

I remember a talk that we had once and the word that he shared with me still sticks with me now. Perseverance.

I watched him build his dream lifestyle and until this day he is still building it. I used to get so upset with him because his mouth can be so reckless at times. But that is what I love the most about him because he is going to tell it like it is and he holds you accountable for your actions.
His sternness has played a major role in my life and business. Just seeing how he handles situations especially business showed me that if you just stay focused, driven and do what it takes to get what you want the sky is the limit.

I commend him because he was the only male in the house and he had his hands full with me and my sister, but he showed us what to expect from a man and how a man should treat us. He is my superman!

I am so grateful that I had an example of sternness in my life to keep me accountable in the pursuit of my goals.

The closeness of family

My grandkids mean the world to me. It has been my mission to show them that you can be and have anything you put your mind to. Therefore, I lead by example. I have learned that children watch you and they are like sponges, absorbing everything. Being around my family causes me to want to stay consistent in striving to be a better person.

My family element is everything because without their love and support I would not have made it this far.

Without those shoulders to lean on, venting sessions with my sisters, cocktails and conversation with family I would have lost my mind. They are my core foundation.

Many times, we would love to say that we are able to do things on our own, but without my family, I know I would have never made it.

INVEST IN YOURSELF

Chapter twelve

INVEST IN YOURSELF

Scared money doesn't make money! That word money is a touchy subject for some and it was very touchy for me when I didn't have it. I knew it took money to make money. I knew that if I wanted to succeed in life I had to take some risk. You do know that God was a risk taker?

Guess what it goes deeper than that before you get the scared money you must be worthy of it. You must earn the scared money, it is not given easily. God must trust you first. Meaning that you must be Faithful over the little things. How can you expect God to bless you with something better when you are not taking of what you have? Another thing I have learned is that God will not bless us when He knows we will not continue to praise nor give Him the Glory. As my Apostle says, "God don't need no part time lover."

Do something that you normally wouldn't do. Get comfortable with being uncomfortable. Dare to dream big and act on it. This book should have come out last year, but I allowed fear to win and put it off. I stepped outside of my comfort zone and said somebody come take me to the labor room because I am about to give birth! I am ready.

I have been carrying this thang too long it is overdue. Here come those cover girls saying Push, Push!

.

Listen to God when He's directing you to make an investment—I had it bad questioning God when he has instructed me to do something. I was like God if this is you, you must show me and boom He showed me.

Investing is not always money. Investing means doing something you have never done to get something you never had. Investing your time in being trained or educated will pay off in the long run. Invest in yourself whether it self-improvement or just being coached, take the time to make sure the investment is what is needed for you to move forward and to get to where it is you are trying to go.

If you want to start a business invest in that. Meaning go to seminars, conventions, and webinars. I took 200 dollars and invested in a trillion-dollar business and I don't regret it at all. I have worked it and now it works for me. You are only as successful as you think you are.

Move in SILENCE

Keep your mouth shut and Let God make the noise. I learned that most people Prey on you instead of Praying for you. You can kill the dream before it becomes a reality by talking too much.

You can abort the birth of your dreams by prematurely speaking too much. Sometimes others will run with your idea when you reveal it to the wrong people. You must be mindful and seek guidance from God. Sometimes we will be so full and want to share but know that we can't release a word until God has given us clearance too. When I started writing this book I wanted to tell the world, but I knew I couldn't until it was fully birthed, so I just contained it. It was hard, but I give all the Glory to God for keeping me through this process.

I heard this statement from one of my Pastor's messages "Lord I don't want to just obtain but contain".

I was speaking of the blessing, never imagining it would be this. God works in wondrous ways! It has happened to me so now I just move in silence. I have learned that when you are quiet and working low key people are trying to figure out what is going on. When you are silent about your moves you are more focused on the task at hand and there is no outside interference. A silent mouth keeps the devil out your business.

Believing in Yourself

When you start believing in yourself your actions will line up with your beliefs. This starts with writing your goals down and making sure that they are attainable. I wrote down both my long and short terms goal with dates. This helped me tremendously to stay focused on them. I had to learn the difference between the two because one can be achieved quicker than the other.

I had to start prioritizing my goals. This was through deciding what is most important right now. Focus mainly on that goal.

You also must be willing to be flexible because as your life changes your goals will begin to change.

Hold yourself accountable

I think that I am my worst critic when it comes to accountability. Accountability is not just a mindset but a skill set. It was hard for me to open up to people, but this helped me in becoming humble. It is humbling when you must give account and be responsible and take ownership of your choices, actions and behavior.

This also helped my self-esteem to grow. I have come to realize that people will respect you, relationships will flourish, and it helps you to be a great example for others to listen to and follow. I hold myself to high standards.

Encourage yourself when others don't! You have to look yourself in the mirror daily and tell yourself Girl you got this!

When others don't celebrate you, celebrate yourself. Put on that little black dress and those gold heels and treat yourself. Self- love is the best love.

You are your biggest and loudest cheerleader. I find myself pumping and priming myself all the time. For me it is music. I love all types of music. We control our atmosphere. Start putting yourself in the atmosphere that will help you to keep pushing.

Show up and show out

Allow God to show up and show out on your behalf. God will announce you to some and reintroduce you to others. God has a way of doing things a lot better than us. As I sit here writing this book I can only smile because I know without a shadow of doubt He is about to Do it Big!

This birthing was not easy, and it was a fight for me to get here. But God! For He knows better than me. I Trust God to do just what he said He will do.

Soaring

Believe that you can achieve, and you will do it!

Keeping the Faith and staying in the fight has been my motto. The fight has been fixed and the victory has been won already. It is up to us to stand our ground. If I would have listened to everyone that said I couldn't do it, I would be still waiting to start.

I remember my professor sending a clip to me from Steve Harvey talking about Jumping. This motivated me to take that leap of Faith. Has it been easy? Of course not! It has however, been rewarding. If anything, this journey has taught me that Persistence, Consistency, and Perseverance are how you will win this race.

Those three things will get you to the finish line. Believing in yourself is the first step, positioning yourself for the dream is the second step and doing what it takes to achieve that dream is the last step.

Well when God decided that I was an entrepreneur, I was like wait a minute how am I going to make it?

Here it is 8 years later. The number 8 represents new beginnings and I am still standing tall. I haven't gone without food, water, a roof over my head, clothes on my back and shoes on my feet. I Trusted God and allowed God to order my steps. When I was doing things on my own it was all jacked up and I didn't have anything. Now I have a favor filled life. God Is faithful.

Take the limits off

I used to say that like I guess, I think, or I settle. God stopped me from doing that. Now I can, I have, and It shall be. With

God there is no limits and He have the final say so in any situation.

Let me share a personal experience with you. The Range Rover is my dream car, so I started doing the research and found out some things that changed my mind. I started looking at G wagons (Mercedes) and I shared it with one of my sisters. She knew someone at a car lot and told me to reach out to them. This certain car lot is very nice and has luxury cars. If your credit isn't right, you will get your feelings hurt. For days I put it off until this one-day God said go to the car lot. I hesitated at first asking God, "Is this You speaking?" I decided to listen and long story short had I not obeyed God I would have missed out on my Blessing.

God is a miracle worker and there are no limits with God. Take the limits off. I don't care what it looks like when god is in it there are no limits.

Flying High

Every brick that they throw at me God used them for the foundation of my predestined elevation, so they can see me soar.

Flying high like an eagle. Soaring the skies. You know eagles glide when they are in the sky. When I look my life over I won't complain. Every single brick that has been thrown at me I am now either walking over or have hung my pictures of success on the wall that was built with those bricks.

My destiny was predetermined before I was born. God already knew that this time would come. It was once stated that I was rough around the edges. Well that statement was very true because I was in the stages of being formed into the diamond that I am today.

Everyone wants to be a diamond, but no one wants to be cut. I was cut and pressed many times before I was shaped in form into this rare and unique person that I am. I am Grateful, and gratefulness is a door to access and remain. Being Thankful will keep you there according 1 Thessalonians 5:18 it states in everything gives Thanks. Our gratitude determines our Blessings.

Leather Chairs

We now sit in leather chairs- I went from jail ceils to leather chairs!

What do I mean by this? Some of you may not have been in jail physically but emotionally, spiritually and in your mind, you have been locked up. Not able to move on your free will, having someone or something control you. See, in that jail ceil is where my dream started! In that jail cell is where I began writing my vision while sitting on the jail ceil floor. Here today I completed my dream sitting in a leather chair. I now sit in leather chairs seeing my dreams turn into reality.

Through it all I remain humble because humility is not being prideful or arrogant. Humility means that I admit to the mistakes, choices, and behavior.

I admit that I need help. Being humble removed Myoshi out of the equation. According to Proverbs 27.2 You should never praise yourself, let others do it.

In that jail ceil I had to be humble to hear instruction. I was granted access to the Leather Chairs to help others with my story of how I made it Against All Odds. God has allowed me to receive these privileges to help and bless others, to teach others and to let others know that if God can do it for me surely, He can for you if you surrender and do the work.

About the Author

Myoshi Robinson - ***Thomas*** *is a National Speaker, Entrepreneur & Author* of the ALL NEW BOOK Against All Odds: From the Jail Cell to Leather Chairs. She is the epitome of "Don't judge a book by its cover" as she has turned a 7-year prison sentence into a global movement to empower others to push forward beyond seemingly catastrophic setbacks.

Myoshi shares her greatest lessons learned in this book, which has opened the doors to entrepreneurship in several companies including Rich Chicks, Inc. and Miracles in Progress. She decided that her past would not define her future, which has also led to becoming the CEO and owner of Two Angels Tax Services and Two Angels Credit Services.

Her story has catapulted Myoshi on stages nationwide where she shares how she has been able to keep going in the face of adversity while teaching others to do the same.

To find out more about Myoshi Robinson – Thomas visit
www.myoshirobinsonthomas.com

www.ingramcontent.com/pod-product-compliance
Ingram Content Group UK Ltd.
Pitfield, Milton Keynes, MK11 3LW, UK
UKHW041939190726
13854UKWH00004B/1688